PROFESSIONAL CAREERS AND

ENTREPRENEURSHIP

PROFESSIONAL CAREERS AND ENTREPRENEURSHIP

A Guide Towards Upward Economic Mobility

C. DONOVAN GRIFFITHS

LYNX PUBLISHERS

ISBN (eBook/Kindle): 979-8-218-72810-6

ISBN (Paperback): 978-1-968012-45-8

ISBN (Hardcover): 978-1-968012-46-5

Library Of Congress Catalog Card Number: 2025919614

Published in the United States of America by Lynx Publishers.

Success is a function of the relentless pursuit of knowledge.

Why, why I wrote this book?

Over the last fifteen years, I have been wrestling with the question of why some ethnic groups enjoyed unbridle prosperity and so much of the world's population are in poverty? And so, I have been on this journey of exploring the cause and effect. My research has clearly and conclusively show that cultural values account for the different outcomes.

On the one hand, groups that embrace a set of progressive cultural values are better off because they are builders. And so, they flourished over time. And the other groups that are steep in ignorance not only destroy and maintain their impoverish status; but in many cases, the future generations are even worst off. So, my purpose is to increase awareness to the fortunate ones who make use of this information. It is my contribution in aiding the reduction of world's poverty.

DEDICATION

*Special Thanks to Carrol Turner and
Monica Baker for their support*

CONTENTS

INTRODUCTION

You have the potential to build the life that you want. So, what will you build?

This career guide in no way intends to undermine the many meaningful occupations in skilled trades or craftsmanship such as plumbers, welders, elevator mechanics, electricians, operating engineers, machinists, carpenters, and many others. **However, the guide focuses on professional careers such as researchers, inventors, designers, builders, and producers.** It is easy to make the case that human progress has largely derived from technological progress. The base layer of technology is ideas that solve big world's problems.

These ideas lead to new technologies or improvement of existing technologies. Many of these innovations not only advance human progress but they also transformed standard of living across the world. Examples are household appliances such as the dishwasher, refrigerator, washing machine, cloth dryer, microwave, etc. The inventors that transform transportation systems like aero planes, trains, automobiles and shipping. The engineers that process earth metal materials into steel that allow the building of high-rise buildings.

The inventors of elevators and electrification allow humans to occupy high rise buildings. The engineers that design the specification that build machines for roads, bridges, tunnels and highways. The inventors of our communication systems that organized languages, built the internet, mobile telephones, television, mailing system, newspapers printing, and books. The medical researchers who discovered cure for diseases and illnesses, the many equipment used to diagnose illnesses. The chemist who develops medications that soothe our aches and pains. The bankers who design and build our financial system so that society can exchange goods and services for fiat currency locally, national and international.

The lawyers who write laws to regulate social and economic conduct of society. I cannot fail to include food researchers, the variety of discoveries in food choices. The sociologist or psychologists that provide insight into human traits and behaviors and so much more. It is noteworthy to mention that just about all the designers and builders had failed over and over in their pursuits. But the ones that succeed never hide behind their failures. They learned and lead in their chosen industry.

It is worthwhile to note that culture is a phenomenal that drive prosperity. In other words, culture is that coherent system of values, attitudes, and institutions that influences individual and social behavior in various dimensions that allow human to succeed. It is the parents or teachers that support and encourage experimentation and constructive criticism that help young individuals to both discover their talent and interest, as well as mesh them. This type of progressive culture embodies inner confidence, and ultimately drive not just innovation, but extraordinary achievement.

MINDSET FOR HIGH ACHIEVEMENT

Developing the mindset for high achievement requires focus and courage where you use your disadvantages as tools to transform them into advantages. Your mind is the command center of your existence. So, it is of utmost important that from birth, if lucky, your social environment fosters a set of values, beliefs, and practices that support and build a positive mind.

According to GROC AI, mindset mastery involves developing the ability to control and utilize one's thoughts and beliefs to achieve the desired outcomes and personal growth. It encompasses the understanding of how mindset impacts behavior; learning to shift negative thought patterns, plus cultivating a positive, growth-oriented attitudes. Mindset of mastery aims to empower individuals to overcome challenges, achieve their goals, and create a life that aligns with their aspirations.

High achievement motive offers numerous benefits, including increased opportunities, personal growth, and satisfaction. High achievement is what drives progress in society, fostering a sense of purpose and accomplishment. It also provides a balance between striving for high standards and maintaining overall well-being. Moreover, high achievement involves developing high-value skills and pushing personal boundaries, which can lead to continuous advancement. The journey of high achievement comes with many twists and turns that must be embraced with courage, resolve, and resilience.

The Strength from Within

As a human, you hold the possibilities of high achievement in your hands. You have the potential to fashion whatever identity you want. But you must build up the mental and emotional resilience through self-awareness and self-care. Besides, you must develop the coping skills for the challenges that you will encounter. You must build the grit, like courage, perseverance, self-sacrifice, determination, optimism, and emotional intelligence to navigate difficult situations. This process involves mindfulness, setting healthy boundaries, and building a supportive relationship.

You must learn and attentively cultivate a culture that allows you to prosper. For example, practice positive self-talk and empowering affirmations to boost our confidence and motivation. You must embrace a set of progressive values that include self-discipline, dedication, and hard work to enable prosperity. Equally important, you must bear in mind that building resilience is a journey, not a destination. Be patient. Be kind to yourself and others where there is no adverse consequence to you.

Preparation that shapes prosperity

It is an easy case to make that parents, particularly mothers, are potentially the most important agents to constructively shape their children's cultural values around the achievement motive. In other words, the parents' beliefs, behavior patterns, or mindset are what determine whether children become high achievers or not. Pertaining to the raising of children, when mothers have high expectations of their children to be high achievers, or having parents that fundamentally understand the process of learning and nurture the desire to succeed, is crucial. Ideally, mother and father should have a plan for developing their children to love high achievement.

According to David McClelland, author of *The Achieving Society,* children's motivation for achievement starts between the ages of five and twelve. He believes that the age of five through twelve is the critical growth period when children start developing the confidence to learn, and the desire to be successful at what they choose to do. Moreover, McClelland's research work showed that mothers naturally have 70 – 75 percent of the influence on their children. So, when mothers are armed with a set of progressive values (self-respect, order, punctuality, responsibility, cleanliness, honesty, discipline, respect for others, respect for the law, the drive to succeed, frugalities), their children will not only absorb those values; but it is easy to share those values and practices with their children.

Ideally, individuals should have a plan and a set of values for developing their children. The plan, in my view, should focus on exposing children to different ideas that can lead to a professional career as the child develops a likeness for a particular discipline. Then the child's interest should be nurtured. Those children who have parents with cultural values that allow success will enjoy the process of learning and ultimately are likely to develop a professional career. But the children who have parents who lack similar cultural values are more likely to fail in developing the discipline to learn and succeed.

Therefore, one can conclude that early career preparation is crucial in developing a professional career because the process is slow and lengthy. But more than worth the effort in the end. This endeavor requires focus on using as much of your time on efforts to strengthen your capabilities in languages, reading and comprehension, mathematics, science, and limited sport activity.

Cultural Values

Cultural values and practices are at the center of human prosperity. Progressive values which pointed to self-respect, order, punctuality, responsibility, cleanliness, honesty, respect for others, respect for the law, the drive to succeed, frugality, delaying gratification, etc. Among these values are what allow various ethnic groups to develop professional careers such as finance, medicine, engineering, law, politics, etc. In fact, progressive values are what enable individuals to be exceptional and ultimately master their profession. Additionally, good cultural values encourage a strong work ethic, saving and investing, having a unified family, and service to their community. Moreover, build a business that not only solves big problems but also advances human living standards.

Self Esteem

Broadly speaking, parents provide the most attentive care to their young children. However, one of the most valuable aspects of parenting is early career preparation. On the list of preparation is building self-esteem. It is one most important aspects of early childhood development. According to **Steven Silbiger**, Author of the *Jewish Phenomenon,* Eastern European mothers sang lullabies to their young babies. These lullabies, also known as cradle songs, provide comfort to their future scholars and leaders as they go to sleep. Additionally, fathers worked long hours to produce professional scholars such as bankers, doctors, lawyers, and engineers.

In other words, self-esteem not only fosters but also nurtures self-respect and self-confidence. Self-esteem actualizes the belief that one's duty is to build a great professional career and the life that he or she deserves. Individuals with a high level of self-esteem not only value themselves, but they also have a strong sense of worthiness and privileges that a professional career affords.

Self-Discipline

Self-discipline is the ability to manage one's behavior, emotions, and desires to achieve one's goals. Even when the situation might be difficult, it is ideal to do what best serves your interests. It involves overcoming temptation or weaknesses to obtain a certain outcome. Self-discipline points to what is important over the long run as opposed to instant gratification. Self-discipline ignores the present pleasure for the reward and privilege to come. Even when the situation may be challenging, self-discipline keep you grounded and steered you to do the things you do not want to do. On the other hand, you may be excited or tempted about a given situation. But self-discipline is the character trait that will prevent you from engaging yourself into activities that may not serve your best interest. In other words, self-discipline can be compared to the key that unlocks the door to personal growth. It is one of the most crucial ingredients in the sandbox for high achievement. The average person who practices self-discipline can rise further and is likely to be more successful than the person with special ability and talents who practices little self-discipline.

Clarity allows you to focus on what adds value to your personal growth; it removes confusion, distraction, and procrastination. So, you can channel your efforts into the things that align with your goals. One effective way to develop clarity is to break up your goals into small steps. Work consistently on each part, little by little, because discipline is one of the strongest types of self-love. It is ignoring present pleasure for a bigger reward to come. Sometimes, it may seem that you are not making any progress. However, over time, with consistent efforts, your goals will materialize.

Social Intelligence

Social skills are the ability to see people in the most realistic light possible. It is what allows you to navigate smoothly through the social environment. Social Intelligence allow individuals to focus on learning and acquiring relevant skills. Success is not attainable without a high level of social intelligence. It is not true mastery and will not last. Let us look deeper into some of the characteristics of social intelligence. For example, being open to change. As you evolve, you will face various situations. More often than not, each situation has cost and benefit. So being able to think critically or view each situation from more than one angle is critical for achieving your goal. You must learn to be adaptable, polite, on time, an active listener, and let your integrity shine. You do not want to undermine yourself with arrogance, such as arguing over every issue; wanting always to be right, or having the feeling of entitlement or special treatment.

Additionally, you do not want to engage in negative behavior such as criticizing, complaining without offering any solutions or not being responsible. You don't want to show any aggressive behavior like undue shouting or yelling, threats or intimidation. Be respectful to others. But more importantly, be respectful to yourself; because your observers, more often than not, can see if you do not respect yourself. When you lack self-respect, you will automatically close the opportunity doors. Do not be eager to indulge in controversial topics such as politics, religion or controversial social issues that are unlikely to benefit you. Learn to be solution oriented; and when you don't have the solution, this is the time to lean in, think the situation through to find a solution. Broadly speaking, you want to maintain an attractive personality and allow your counterparts to be comfortable around you..

SCIENCE

Science is a systematic study of various related disciplines. The disciplines of scientific systems build and organize knowledge in the form of testable methods and predictions about the universe. Modern science is typically divided into three major branches that consist of natural science, which is the study of the physical world, such as physics, chemistry, and biology. The social sciences, which study individuals and societies, include economics, psychology, and sociology.

Applied sciences focus on the use of scientific knowledge for practical purposes such as engineering and medicine. Additionally, it is important to include related sciences such as Formal Sciences that focus on the study of logic, mathematics, computer science, deductive reasoning, and empirical evidence. Here, I have provided some major career opportunities.

Life Science Physician Specializations

The highest paid salaries are specialists in surgical and procedural medicine.

Neurosurgeon

Perform surgeries on brain tumors, spinal cord, and related nerve conditions.

Education:	Medical Doctor license, Residency, Fellowship
Salary/Range:	$750,000

Orthopedic Surgeon

Diagnoses, treats, and operates on patients with musculoskeletal issues or injuries.

Education:	Medical Doctor license, Residency, Fellowship
Salary/Range:	$280,000 - $450,000

Orthodontist

Realign teeth and jaws, treating gum diseases, dental malfunctions, and remedies.

Education: *(entry-level)*	Bachelor's Degree in Dental Science and Residency
Salary/Range:	$290,000 - $350,000

Anesthesiologist

Administering anesthesia and managing patient care before, during, and after surgery.

Education:	Bachelor's degree, medical school degree, and residency/fellowship
Salary/Range:	$350,000 - $450,000

Urologist

Specialized in diagnosing and treating disorders of the urinary tracts of males and females, and the reproductive system of males.

Education:	Bachelor's degree, medical school degree, and residency/fellowship
Salary/Range:	$350,000 - $500,000

Family Medicine

A primary care doctor diagnoses and treats a wide range of illnesses and injuries across all age groups within a family, including routine checkups, preventive care, health screenings, and managing chronic conditions.

Education:	Bachelor's degree, medical school degree, and residency/fellowship
Salary/Range:	$250,000 - $275,000

Obstetricians and Gynecologists (OB/GYN)

Medical care during pregnancy or childbirth. Diagnose and treat cancer diseases in the women's reproductive system.

Education:	Bachelor's degree, medical school degree, and residency/fellowship
Salary/Range:	$250,000 - $350,000

Neurologist

Diagnosis and treatment of disorders impacting the brain, spinal cord, and nervous system.

Education:	Bachelor's degree, medical degree at an Allopathic or Osteopathic college, residency/fellowship
Salary/Range:	$300,000 - $500,000

Radiologist

Analyzing medical images to diagnose and treat illnesses. Review ultrasounds, magnetic resonance imaging (MRI), and computed tomography.

Education:	Bachelor's degree, medical school degree, and residency/fellowship
Salary/Range:	$300,000 - 500,000

Oncologist

A physician specializes in diagnosing, treating, and removing cancer tumors.

Education:	Medical doctor
Salary/Range:	$250,000 - $350,000

Cardiologist

Specialized in diagnosing and treating a wide range of heart and blood vessel-related illnesses.

Education:	Bachelor's degree, medical school degree, residency/fellowship
Salary/Range:	$350,000 - $550,000

Gastroenterologist

Specialized in diagnosing and treating the digestive tract, gallbladder, liver, bile ducts, and pancreas.

Education:	Bachelor's degree, medical school degree, residency/fellowship
Salary/Range:	$350,000 - $500,000

Clinical Research Scientist

Conduct diseases experiments, identify cause of infectious diseases, and remedies.

Education:	Master's degree in clinical Pathology
Salary/Range:	$150,000 - $250,000

Ophthalmologist

Medical and surgical care of the eyes and vision; eye and vision services on glasses and contact lenses.

Education:	Bachelor's degree, medical school degree, residency/fellowship
Salary/Range:	$350,000 - $450,000

Pulmonologist

Diagnosing and treating diseases of the respiratory system, including the lungs, airways, and blood vessels, which can cause sleep apnea, fibrosis, etc.

Education:	Bachelor's degree, medical degree, residency, and fellowship
Salary/Range:	$300,000 - $400,000

General Surgeon

Diagnoses and treats a wide range of diseases in human bodies, such as appendectomies, bowel repairs, gallbladder surgery, hernia surgery, colonoscopy, gastric bypass, thyroidectomy, traumas, and critical care.

Education:	Bachelor's degree, medical degree, residency, and fellowship
Salary/Range:	$375,000 - 425,000

Pathologist

Performed and analyzed autopsies, infectious diseases, body tissues/body fluids.

Education:	Bachelor of Science degree, medical degree, Pathology residency, fellowship in pathology.
Salary/Range:	$300,000 - $350,000

Psychiatrist

Diagnose and treat mental, emotional, and behavioral disorders.

Education:	Bachelor's degree in psychology, medical degree, and residency program
Salary/Range:	$275,000 - $375,000

Physical Therapist

Helps patients recover from injuries, manage pain, and improve physical function through prescribed exercises, hands-on care, and patient education

Education:	Bachelor's degree, Doctor of Physical Therapy, State License
Salary/Range:	$115,000 - $135,000

Chiropractor

Diagnose and treat patients with musculoskeletal issues, such as injuries to the spine, muscles, ligaments, and joints, using manual therapies and lifestyle and exercise. Create treatment plans and often refer patients to various medical specialists when necessary.

Education:	Bachelor's, Doctor of Chiropractic degrees, & State License
Salary/Range:	$120,000 - $150,000

Pediatrics

Specializing in children's health from birth to young adulthood.

Education:	Bachelor's degree, medical degree, pediatrics residency, and fellowship
Salary/Range:	$200,000 - $250,000

ENGINEERING/SCIENTIST

It's important to note that a PhD is the highest level of study and stands for Doctor of Philosophy. It does not necessarily mean that one has a doctorate degree in philosophy. Here, in this context, the philosophy part refers to the Greek word meaning *love of wisdom*. You can get a Ph.D. in any subject, including, but not limited to, engineering, chemistry, computer science, biology, physics, as well as social science, political science, anthropology, literature, business, and environmental design, etc.

Getting a doctorate degree takes, in general, between six and ten years, depending on the field of study. Upon acceptance into a program, students are called doctoral or Ph.D. students. The initial requirements include coursework and comprehensive examinations. Once the exams are completed, they are often referred to as a Ph.D. candidate. The next steps are conducting original research and then putting the research into a thesis – also called a dissertation – that is written and then defended orally before a supervisory panel of experts.

Biomedical Scientist

Conduct and analyze laboratory test results on patients' samples, ensuring compliance with health and safety regulations, and conduct research for the advancement of medical science.

Education:	Bachelor's, master's, and Ph.D. degrees
Salary/Range:	$115,000 - $140,000

Medical Scientist

Conduct clinical trials, working with doctors to test treatment on patients who have agreed to participate in a clinical study.

Education:	Bachelor's, master's, and Ph.D. degrees
Salary/Range:	$170,000 - $260,000

Biologist Scientist

Studies living organisms, such as humans, animals, and plants. Biological investigation shows how these different organisms' function, adapt, and evolve in their environments.

Education:	Bachelor's, master's, and Ph.D. degrees
Salary/Range:	$95,000 - $130,000

Marine Biologist

Studies the behavior of ocean organisms, engages in conservation efforts, education, aquariums, and research reports, etc.

Education:	Bachelor's, master's, and Ph.D. degrees.
Salary/Range:	$100,000 - $125,000

Forensic Biologist

Specializes in applying biological knowledge and principles to assist in criminal and civil investigations. Typically work directly for law enforcement agencies or private forensic analysis in hospitals, universities, etc.

Education:	Bachelor's, master's, and Ph.D. degrees
Salary/Range:	$97,000 - $135,000

Marine Scientist

Studies marine life, seafloors, coastal areas, and the atmosphere. Conduct research to understand the ocean's physical, chemical, and geological properties, as well as the behavior and interactions of marine organisms. The gain of knowledge helps inform policy decisions and management practices related to ocean conservation and management.

Education:	Bachelor's, master's, and Ph.D. degrees
Salary/Range:	$143,000 - $155,000

Botanist Scientist

Studies plants to understand structure, growth, reproduction, and interaction with their environment. Conduct research for institutions such as universities, botanical gardens, museums, and private industry, focusing on areas like conservation, agriculture, and environmental protection.

Education:	Bachelor's, master's, and Ph.D. degrees
Salary/Range:	$95,000 - $125,000

Ecologist

Studies the relationships between living organisms and their environment, often focusing on how human actions impact ecosystems and biodiversity. Used data analysis, field research, and scientific knowledge to address environmental problems, develop conservation strategies, and advise on ecological polices.

Education:	Bachelor's, master's, and Ph.D. degrees
Salary/Range:	$75,000 - $125,000

Microbiologist

Specializes in living organisms that can only be seen with the aid of a microscope. Typically conduct research for colleges, universities, pharmaceutical companies, and agricultural producers, etc.

Education:	Bachelor's, master's, and Ph.D. degrees
Salary/Range:	$95,000 - $125,000

Molecular Biologist

Study and analyze plant, animal, or human genetics and their relationships with each other. They often study DNA and RNA of living organisms and combine chemistry, physiology, genetics, and physics within their research.

Education:	Bachelor's, master's, and Ph.D. in Biological studies
Salary/Range:	$110,000 - $140,000

23

Medical Laboratory Scientist

Analyzing blood, body fluids, tissues, & cells. Relaying test results to physicians. Utilizing microscopes, cell counters, and high-precision lab equipment.

Education:	Bachelor's, master's, and Ph.D. degrees
Salary/Range:	$105,000 - $135,000

Clinical Pharmaceutical Scientist

Engage in drug formulation, analysis of clinical trials to evaluate the safety and efficacy of pharmacological properties, medical devices, and therapeutic treatments.

Education:	Bachelor's, master's, and Ph.D. degrees
Salary/Range:	$110,000 - $125,000

Clinical Geneticist

Studies inheritance and genetic variation in living organisms, often specializing in research, diagnosis, or treatment of genetic disorders. Analyze genetic data, conduct experiments, and interpret laboratory results to understand how genes influence traits and health.

Education:	Bachelor's, master's, Ph.D., and or Medical Doctor degree
Salary/Range:	$190,000 - $200,000

Neuroscientist

Research focuses on understanding the function of the human brain and the peripheral nervous system that controls animals' and humans' senses, behavior, and thought processes.

Education:	Bachelor's, master's, Ph.D., and Physician License
Salary/Range:	$500,000 - $750,000

Food Scientist

Use of chemistry, biology, and other related sciences to study the basic elements of food. Analyze nutritional content of food, discover new food sources, and research ways to make processed foods safe and healthy.

Education:	Bachelor's, master's, and Ph.D. degrees
Salary/Range:	$80,000 - $125,000

Food Chemist

Studies chemical composition and reactions within food, aiming to improve its quality, safety, and nutritional value. Analyze and improve food products and develop new food formulations. Research new methods for food preservation and innovative processing.

Education:	Bachelor's, master's, Ph.D. degrees
Salary/Range:	$125,000 - $145,000

Nutritionist

Evaluate clients' needs, education, and counseling on nutrition and healthy eating habits, and develop a personalized nutrition plan for clients to achieve their goals. Often work in hospitals, clinics, schools, or private practices.

Education:	Bachelor's, master's degrees, Registered Dietitian Nutritionist (RDN) or Certified Nutrition Specialist CNS)
Salary/Range:	$80,000 - $100,000

Applied Science

Engineering ranks among the highest-paid careers due to the need for technological innovation and development. Petroleum engineers are among the highest-paid professionals. High demand for computer science.

Architects

Plan, design, and oversee the construction of houses, factories, office buildings, and other types of building structures.

Education:	Bachelor's, master's degree
Salary/Range:	$122,000 - $160,000

Land-scape Architects

Assess, design, and plan outdoor spaces, focusing on both aesthetics and functionality. Create public and private spaces like parks, gardens, playgrounds, and residential areas, considering factors like park placement, roads, walkways, and building locations.

Education:	Bachelor's, master's degrees
Salary/Range:	$107,000 - $132,000

Aerospace Engineering

Work Description: Design, develop, and test aircraft, spacecraft, satellites, and missiles

Education:	Bachelor's, master's degrees
Salary/Range:	$140,000 - $175,000

Agricultural Engineers

Design farm equipment, planning, managing agricultural product processes, advising farmers, researching crop diseases, and environmental impact assessment.

Education:	Bachelor's, master's degrees
Salary/Range:	$82,000 - $103,000

Bioengineering/Biomedical Engineering

Combine science with design and development of equipment, devices, computer systems, and software.

Education:	Bachelor's, master's degree
Salary/Range:	$106,000 - $162,000

Nuclear Engineering

Designs, builds, and operates nuclear power plants to generate electricity.

Education:	Bachelor's, master's, Professional License, PhD degree
Salary/Range:	$125,000 - $175,000

Communication/Broadcasting Engineer

Design and develop communication equipment and facility systems for long-range functionality, such as circuit design, electronic switching systems, mobile communication, optical fiber cabling, Internet protocol networks, microwave transmission systems, radio and television networks, etc.

Education:	Bachelor's, master's, and Ph.D. degrees
Salary/Range:	$120,000 - $143,000

Geospatial Information System Engineer/Scientist

Using geographic data and technologies such as GIS and GPS to analyze maps on the Earth's surface for various applications, for example, urban planning, environmental management, and disaster response.

Education:	Bachelor's, master's degree, Ph.D.
Salary/Range:	$95,000.00 - $175,000

Meteorologist

Using a mathematical model to analyze and predict the Earth's atmospheric conditions to provide daily weather reports, including climatic patterns.

Education:	Bachelor's, master's degree
Salary/Range:	$97,000 - $120,000

Mining and Geological Engineers

Explore, plan, and manage mines to safely and efficiently remove minerals for manufacturing finished products such as steel, copper, gold, silver, uranium, etc.

Education:	Bachelor's, master's degree
Salary/Range:	$115,000 - $160,000

Petroleum Engineering

Explore, plan, and manage oil & gas well drilling programs, and estimate the quantity

Education:	Bachelor of Science degree, Master's, and Ph.D. degrees
Salary/Range:	$135,000 - $225,000

Petroleum Geologist

Use of geology, geophysics principles, and other scientific methods to explore for oil and natural gas, guiding drilling and production operations. Analyze rock formations, rock sampling, seismic data, and other geological data to identify potential reserves, determine the best locations for drilling wells, and assess the viability of potential reservoirs.

Education:	Bachelor's, master's, Ph.D.
Salary/Range:	$135,000 - $155,000

Computer Science Engineering

Design software, hardware design, architecture, coding, programming, and operating systems

Education:	Bachelor's degree, Master's/P h D degree
Salary/Range:	$125,000 - $175,000

Industrial Engineering

Design, analyze, and improve the system to increase productivity, reduce cost, and increase efficiency.

Education:	Bachelor of Science degree, Master's, and PhD
Salary/Range:	$110,000 - $135,000

Geodesist Engineer/Scientist

Analyzes the Earth's shape, gravitational field, the Earth's rotation, and the evolution in time

Education:	Bachelor's, master's degree
Salary/Range:	$100,000 - $130,000

Physicist

Research principles that influence matter and energy, conduct experiments in technologies, medicine, energy, and other related fields.

Education:	Bachelor's, Master 's, Ph.D.
Salary/Range:	$126,000 - $242,000

Bioinformatics Engineering/Scientist

Analyze biological data, develop software and algorithms, research in genomics, proteomics, and understanding and interpreting complex biological information.

Education:	Bachelor's, Ph.D. degrees in biology, computer science, or bioinformatics
Salary/Range:	$115,000 - $135,000

Hydrologist Engineer

Analyze the movement and distribution of water quality using scientific methods and data, understanding and managing water resources, addressing environmental issues, and designing water-related infrastructure.

Education:	Bachelor's and Ph.D. degrees
Salary/Range:	$95,000 - $140,000

Robotics Engineering

Designs, builds, and configures robotic systems, applying principles from mechanical, electrical, and computer science that allow integration of components like sensors, actuators, motors, and controller arms to create automated tasks in various industries.

Education:	Bachelor's, master's, or PhD degree in a related field such as computer science, robotics, electrical, or mechanical engineering
Salary/Range:	$105,000 - $155,000

Electrical Engineering/Scientist

Conduct research, design, test, and supervise the manufacturing of electrical components.

Education:	Bachelor of Science degree, Master's, and PhD
Salary/Range:	$125,000 - $210,000

System Analysis

Analyzes business performance, with the aim of improving efficiency and productivity.

Education:	Bachelor's, master's degree in computer science
Salary/Range:	$110,000 - $135,000

Automotive Engineering

Designing, developing, and improving component systems in various types of motor vehicles.

Education:	Bachelor's, master's degree in automotive/materials science/or electrical or mechanical engineering
Salary/Range:	$105,000 - $150,000

Material Science Engineering

Develop, process, and test the quality of materials used to create various products such as computer chips, aircraft, golf clubs, etc.

Education:	Bachelor's degree in Material science (Study mechanical, physical, and chemical properties of various materials, such as metals, composites, nanomaterials, etc.) Internship, Professional Engineer License (PE), master's, and Ph.D. degrees are optional
Salary/Range:	$98,000 - $180,000

Mechatronics Engineering

Engineers research, design, and combine mechanical, electronic, and computer engineering to build intelligent machines and devices to improve the production of goods and services.

Education:	Bachelor's degree in Engineering Science, master's degree, PhD
Salary/Range:	$100,000 - $180,000

Civil Engineering

Designs, builds, maintains, and operates infrastructure projects and systems, such as roads, bridges, buildings, and water treatment plants for public and private sectors.

Education:	Bachelor's degree, master's degree, PhD
Salary/Range:	$116,000 - $132,000

Chemist Professional

Analyzing, synthesizing chemical compounds, conducting experiments, and developing new products or processes. Improving existing products to enhance efficiency and quality. Using various analytical techniques such as spectroscopy, chromatography, and wet chemistry methods

Education:	Bachelor's, master's, and PhD degrees
Salary/Range:	$95 000 - $150,000

Marine Engineering

Design, build, and maintain engine and mechanical systems on ships and marine vessels.

Education:	Bachelor's degree in marine engineering
Salary/Range:	$116,000 - $142,000

Chemical Engineering

Design, develop, and optimize chemical manufacturing processes, applying principles of chemistry and physics to produce goods in industries such as pharmaceutical, energy, and many other industries.

Education:	Bachelor's, master's, and PhD degrees.
Salary/Range:	$112,000 - $135,000

Manufacturing Engineering

Designing, implementing, and optimizing manufacturing processes in factories. Researching and developing new equipment and procedures to maximize efficiency, ensure quality standards, and minimize cost.

Education:	Bachelor's, master's degree/Certified Manufacturing Engineer
Salary/Range:	$105,000 - $130,000

Environmental Scientist

Researches, analyzes environmental risk, data collection, develops solutions, ensures regulatory compliance, and develops policy to ensure safety and security.

Education:	Bachelor's, master's, and Ph.D. degrees
Salary/Range:	$127,000 - $145,000

Cybersecurity Specialist

Protects the organization's computer systems and networks from cyberattacks, ensuring data confidentiality and integrity, and implementing security measures, monitoring, and responding to security threats.

Education:	Bachelor's, master's degree in computer science & cybersecurity
Salary/Range:	$145,000 - $190,000

Cartographers and Photogrammetrists

Collect, analyze, and interpret geographic information to create and update the location of maps.

Education:	Bachelor's, master's degree
Salary/Range:	$80,000 - $110,000

Landscape Architect

Designs and oversees outdoor space for aesthetic and functional purposes, such as homes, parks, gardens, college campuses, etc.

Education:	Bachelor's, master's degree
Salary/Range:	$108,000 - $125,000

Veterinarian

Examine and treat various medical conditions in house pets, agricultural animals, zoos, etc.

Education:	Bachelor's, Doctor of Veterinary Medicine (DVM)
Salary/Range:	$140,000 - $201,000

Renewable Energy Engineer

Design, implement, and maintain renewable energy infrastructure such as solar, wind, and hydro power, research and develop new technologies and processes.

Education:	Bachelor's, master's degree
Salary/Range:	$115,000 - $130,000

Earth Science

Geologist

Study the Earth's composition, structure, and processes to understand its history and natural resources such as petroleum, oil, gas, and rare earth materials. They collect data, analyze samples, and interpret geological information to make informed decisions related to resource extraction, environmental management, and natural hazard assessment, such as earthquakes, volcanoes, tsunamis, etc. Fieldwork, laboratory analysis, and research are conducted for various industries.

Education:	Bachelor's, Master's, and Ph.D. degrees
Salary/Range:	$85,000 - $150,000

Geoscientist

Study the Earth that relates to a wide range of fields that include geology, geophysics, geochemistry, and environmental science. They use various methods such as fieldwork, lab analysis, and remote sensing devices to investigate the Earth's layers, rocks, fossils, and natural resources. They also develop geological models, analyze data, identify, and manage natural resources.

Education:	Bachelor's, master's, and Ph.D. degrees
Salary/Range:	$110,000 - $170,000

Carto-graphist

Collect spatial data from sources like aerial photographs, satellite imagery, and ground surveys to produce maps.

Education:	Bachelor's, master's degrees
Salary/Range:	$95,000 - $121,000

Petroleum Geologist

Use geological knowledge to explore and extract oil and natural gas, analyze various rock formations and seismic data to identify other geological resources.

Education:	Bachelor's, master's, and Ph.D. degrees
Salary/Range:	$90,000 - $130,000

Photogrammetrist

Collects and analyzes spatial data that includes aerial photos, satellite imagery.

Education:	Bachelor's and master's degrees
Salary/Range:	$110,000 - $140,000

Geodesist/Engineering

Measuring and monitoring the Earth's size, shape, and gravitational field, surveying, and remote sensing such as InSAR (Interferometric Synthetic Aperture Radar)

Education:	Bachelor's, master's degrees
Salary/Range:	$110,000 - $145,000

Hydro-graphist

Conduct surveying and mapping of oceans and seas, create nautical charts which are essential for safe navigation of ships and boats, dredging projects, and infrastructure development, including offshore wind farms, oil rigs, and subsea cables.

Education:	Bachelor's, master's degree, and industry certification
Salary/Range:	$90,000 - $130,000

Shipwright Engineer

Design and construct ships, boats, submarines, and water sports vessels.

Education:	Bachelor's, master's degrees
Salary/Range:	$110,000 - $140,000

Computational Science

Computational Scientist

Conduct simulation and modeling in various fields, explore and test theories that often lead to the discovery, development, and adoption of new technologies. Use of computational models to solve problems, test, and evaluate mathematical, statistical, and computer-simulated models. analyzing data, developing algorithms, and creating new software tools.

Education:	Bachelor's, master's, and Ph.D.
Salary/Range:	$175 000 - $225,000

Mathematician

Use knowledge of mathematics to solve problems in various industries, academia, and government that involve numbers, data, quantity, structure, space, models, and change.

Education:	Bachelor's, master's, and Ph.D.
Salary/Range:	$120,000 - $190,000

Statistician

Collecting and analyzing data to identify trends and patterns to make informed decisions in various industries. The data is often provided in charts and graphs to communicate findings.

Education:	Bachelor's, master's degrees, and certification
Salary/Range:	$98,000 - $120,000

Actuary Science

Data collection for measuring and managing risk in finance, insurance, and human behavior

Education:	Bachelor's, master's degrees, and certifications
Salary/Range:	$127,000 - $200,000

Web and Digital Interface Designers

Designing the look and feel of websites and digital products, ensuring websites are visually appealing and easy to use; creating graphics, testing interfaces, and optimizing websites for performance and marketability; optimizing the design for performance and mobile compatibility

Education:	Bachelor's or master's degree in computer science.
Salary/Range:	$125,000 - $176,000

General Scientific Occupations

Forensic Scientist

Analyze data or traces of evidence in various industries such as legal investigations, medical reports, DNA research (Deoxyribonucleic acid), etc.

Education:	Bachelor's, master's degrees, and certification
Salary/Range:	$110,000 - $130,000

Government Scientist

Conduct research to advance future technological innovation, contribute to the development of scientific policies, manage scientific programs, and communicate with policymakers and the public.

Education:	Bachelor's, master's, and Ph.D. degrees
Salary/Range:	$120,000 - 150,000

Inventor

Create new ways to produce a product or service, often improve old methods, or build new industries that advance human living standards.

Education:	Bachelor's, master's, degrees, or driven with a high achievement motive
Salary/Range:	$115,000 - $140,000

Healthcare Scientist

Use the body of knowledge and experience to improve healthcare standards. Conduct research in medical institutions such as hospitals and pharmaceutical and medical equipment producing companies, focusing on areas such as disease prevention, clinical trials, and developing new ways to conduct diagnostic techniques.

Education:	Bachelor's, master's, Ph.D./License Medical Doctor
Salary/Range:	$180,000 - $350,000

Healthcare Administrator

Manage daily operation of healthcare facilities like nursing homes and assisted living facilities, staffing and oversight of staff, financial budget and planning, such as patient fees and billing, employee payroll/benefits, compliance with state laws, focusing on patient care and operational efficiency.

Education:	Bachelor's and master's degrees
Salary/Range:	$122,000 - $142,000

Science Attaché

Member of a diplomatic team who advises on scientific and technical matters, reports on existing and new scientific standards, or natural resource development.

Education:	Bachelor's, master's, and Ph.D.
Salary/Range:	$120,000 - $185,000

Natural science

Archaeologist

Study and analyze artifacts of animals and people from historical sites, often via fieldwork excavation, conduct research reports, and curate exhibits.

Education:	Bachelor's, master's, and Ph.D. degrees
Salary/Range:	$85,000 - $110,000

Astronaut

Use spacecraft to explore space or conduct research beyond the Earth's atmosphere. The research often led to new technologies that advance human living standards.

Education:	Bachelor's, master's, and Ph.D. degrees
Salary/Range:	$150,000 - $175,000

Biochemical Engineer

A combination of chemistry and biology that maximizes the processing in industries like pharmaceutical production, food processing, biofuels, and the study of how various living organisms evolve, and material processing.

Education:	Bachelor's, master's, Ph.D./industry certification
Salary/Range:	$110,000 - $210,000

Aeronautical /Aviation Engineer

Design and construction of aircraft, helicopters, and drones.

Education:	Bachelor's, master's, and Ph.D.
Salary/Range:	$95,000 - $110,000

Astronomer Scientist

Studies planets or atmospheres beyond Earth. such as stars, the moon, and other galaxies to identify patterns and relationships in the universe.

Education:	Bachelor's, master's, Ph.D. degrees
Salary/Range:	$130,000 - $190,000

Electro-chemical Engineer

Involves research and development that focuses on electricity and chemical reactions. Conduct experiments and potentially develop new technologies such as new micro-processors, transformers, battery technologies, fuel cells, solar panels, etc.

Education:	Bachelor's, master's, Ph.D. degrees
Salary/Range:	$110,000 - $140,000

Research Engineer

Involve in the practical implementation of ideas, building prototypes, and exploring and testing new technologies.

Education:	Bachelor's, master's, and Ph.D.
Salary/Range:	$110,000 - $245,000

Food Chemist

Formulate new food products and processes, analyze ingredients' reactions, and improve the composition of food and beverages to ensure safety, quality, and repeat consumption. Focus on flavor, texture, and shelf life.

Education:	Bachelor's, master's, and Ph.D. degrees
Salary/Range:	$110,000 - $135,000

Wildlife Biologist

Studies wild animals and their habitats, focusing on their behavior, genetics, population dynamics, and their survival interactions within their environment. Track animal movements, conservation programs, research reports, and public educational programs

Education:	Bachelor's and master's degrees
Salary/Range:	$80,000 - $105,000

Molecular Geneticist

Study and analyze gene data that focuses on heredity and inheritance traits in living organisms. Conduct experiments, write reports, develop protocols to improve existing genetic techniques, and develop new diagnostic procedures, devising methods to modify gene traits, as well as a breeding program for endangered species.

Education:	Bachelor's, master's, and Ph.D. degrees
Salary/Range:	$120,000 - $150,000

Oceanographer

Studies and analyzes biological properties of the oceans and the processes that govern them, investigates the ocean's currents, temperatures, salinity, chemistry, and its impact on weather and climate. Monitor and interpret ocean data from satellites and remote sensing technology, as well as water and sediment sampling, measure currents, waves, tides, and seawater movements.

Education:	Bachelor's, master's, Ph.D. degrees
Salary/Range:	$95,000 - $150,000

Computational Biologist

Use of computation and statistical methods to analyze biological data, develop models, and extract insights from large datasets, which include DNA sequences, protein structures, and gene expression patterns. Research often leads to new therapies or treatments.

Education:	Bachelor's, master's, and Ph.D.
Salary/Range:	$95,000 - $135,000

Biotechnologist

Design and optimize biological processes for various applications, analyze experimental data, and ensure safety protocols are followed. Often conduct research in stem cell, cancer, virology, genetics, biochemistry, and pharmacology.

Education:	Bachelor's, master's, and Ph.D. degrees
Salary/Range:	$115,000 - $157,000

Clinical Immunologist

Diagnoses, treats, and manages diseases and conditions related to the immune system, including allergies, autoimmune diseases, and immunodeficiencies.

Education:	Bachelor's, M.D. (medical doctor).
Salary/Range:	$235,000 - $365,000

Pharmacologist

Research the effects of drugs and other chemicals on biological systems through clinical trials, drug development, and explore potential side effects, safe usage, and regulatory compliance.

Education:	Bachelor's, master's, and Ph.D. degrees
Salary/Range:	$142,000 - $180,000

Geographer

Studies and analyzes the Earth's landscapes, the pattern of people, and relationships. Gather data through field observations, maps, satellite imagery, and census data. Advisory to state officials, policy makers on urban planning, resource management, and environmental protection.

Education:	Bachelor's, master's, Ph.D. degrees/ certification
Salary/Range:	$95,000 - $130,000

Sales Engineer

Use engineering knowledge to drive sales and build customer relationships; combine sales skills with technical expertise to understand customer needs, present solutions; provide technical-support to product development.

Education:	Bachelor's, master's degrees
Salary/Range:	$120,000 - $202,000

Sales Representatives of the Manufacturer

Sell products and services to businesses and government agencies, seek new customers, explain benefits of products and services, negotiate prices, answer questions, provide training, and offer post-sale support.

Education:	Bachelor's, Master's degrees
Salary/Range:	$105,000 - $130,000

Airline Pilot

Pre-flight checks of aircraft systems to ensure aircraft take off, flight, and landing are safe and efficient; execute flight routes, review the weather report, communicate with air traffic control, coordinate with co-pilots and cabin crew, and provide updates to passengers.

Education:	Bachelor's degree in Aeronautical Science, commercial pilot license.
Salary/Range:	$226,000 - $550,000

Commercial/Private Aircraft Pilot

Operate aircraft for various tasks such as private transporting, transporting public passengers, cargo, aerial photography, crop dusting; flight preparation includes reviewing weather reports, checking aircraft instruments and systems, communicating with air traffic control and flight support team, and aviation regulation and safety protocols; execute flight route and plan.

Education:	Bachelor's degree in aviation, aeronautical science, and a commercial pilot license
Salary/Range:	$150,000 - $300,000

Flight Engineer/Aircraft Systems Engineer

Mainly conduct pre- and post-flight inspections to ensure the aircraft is in safe and efficient working conditions; monitor that weight and balance are within acceptable limits for safe flight; often serve as first officer on flight, and can pilot the aircraft if the pilot becomes incapacitated.

Education:	Bachelor's, master's degrees in related fields of aeronautical, mechanical, or electrical engineering, Flight Engineer License (FAA), or commercial pilot's License.
Salary/Range:	$120,000 - $220,000

Air Traffic Controllers

Ensures safe and efficient movement of aircraft in the airspace by monitoring their position, speed, and altitude, and communicating with pilots via radio and monitoring aircraft with radar systems; ensuring safe distances and managing the flow of traffic to minimize delays; provides clearance for takeoff and landing.

Education:	Bachelor's degree in an aviation-related field and certified by the Federal Aviation Administration (FAA)
Salary/Range:	$144,000 - $180,000

Ship Captain

Responsible for safe and efficient operation; oversee navigation, crew management; ensure the well-being of passengers, crew, and cargo; execute planned routes, communicate with port authority's personnel and home office, comply with all relevant regulations and procedures

Education:	Bachelor's degree in marine engineering, master's mariner certificate of competency.
Salary/Range:	$121,000 - $230,000

SOCIAL SCIENCE

Anthropologist

Studies different human societies through language, cultural behaviors/social structure, beliefs, biology, focusing on evolution, genetics, material remains and artifacts, conducts research, and analyzes patterns of diverse communities and cultures.

Education:	Bachelor's, master's, and Ph.D.
Salary/Range:	$85,000 - $105,000

Human Resource Manager

Manage the HR department of an organization, including recruiting of staff, maintaining employee records, payroll, and benefits processing.

Education:	Bachelor's and master's degrees
Salary/Range:	$118,000 - $130,000

Journalist

Gathers, writes, and presents news and information to the public about current events such as politics, sports, business, and other topics through various media outlets.

Education:	Bachelor's, master's, Ph.D. degrees
Salary/Range:	$85,000 - $110,000

Editor

Plan, review, and revise content for publication, ensuring accuracy, clarity, and consistency; work with writers to improve the quality of their work and make it suitable for the target audience; often specialize in areas like book editing, content editing, proofreading, or managing editorial operations.

Education:	Master's, Ph.D. degree
Salary/Range:	$88,000 - $130,000

Television News Anchor/Reporter

Presents news stories and current events to the public, often in a studio setting, and reports live from the field; collaborates with producers and reporters to prepare and organize news segments.

Education:	Bachelor's, master's degrees
Salary/Range:	$95,000 - $200,000

Television Talk Show Host/Radio Personality

Conduct engaging radio and television programs by interviewing guests, often in sports, performing arts, politics, and commercials.

Education:	Bachelor's degree - varies
Salary/Range:	$75,000 – millions

Movie Director/Editor

Creates and oversees the creative aspects of a film, from casting to directing actors and ensuring a consistent visual and artistic style; often manages the logistics and finances, ensuring the film stays on schedule and within budget.

Education:	Bachelor's, master's degrees
Salary/Range:	$100,000 - $160,000/(in many cases, in the millions)

Economist

Advise businesses, governments, and individuals on market trends and economic conditions, and develop models that predict future economic growth or recession based on fiscal and monetary policies that relate to inflation, interest rates, and employment.

Education:	Bachelor's, master's degree
Salary/Range:	$110,000 - $135,000

Political Scientist

Involves researching, analyzing, and interpreting data that relates to political systems, polices, and behavior trends and patterns, often focusing on public policy, international relations, or comparative politics.

Education:	Master's, Ph.D. degrees
Salary/Range:	$135,000 - $167,000

Sociologist

Analyze human behavior through past history, conduct interviews, and observations; often drawing conclusions from social identities, trends, and patterns.

Education:	Bachelor's, master's degree
Salary/Range:	$110,000 - $135,000

Linguist

Studying, analyzing language structures, origins, translation, and evolution. For example, phonetics (sounds), syntax (grammar), semantics, or sociolinguistics (language in groups)

Education:	Bachelor's, master's, and Ph.D. degrees
Salary/Range:	$98,000 - $145,000

Industrial Psychologist

Analyze the behavior of organizational workers, enhance effective productivity and employee wellbeing, such as cultural values, and standards for employers and employees.

Education:	Master's and Ph.D. degrees
Salary/Range:	$147,000 - $165,000

Urban Planner

Develop planning for the physical, social, and economic development of cities, towns, and urban areas; create and enforce zoning regulations, manage land use, design infrastructure to address community needs, and guide growth.

Education:	Master's and Ph.D. degrees
Salary/Range:	$85,000 - $110,000

Research Scientist

Conduct experiments and develop original ideas or improve existing ideas, often contributing to the advancement of knowledge in specific fields, and publishing research findings.

Education:	Bachelor's, master's, and Ph.D. degrees
Salary/Range:	$140,000 – $240,000

Author/Writer

Write, edit, and analyze written material on various topics such as creative writing (fiction) and non-fiction, educational, classical literature, etc., and prepare writing work for publication.

Education:	Bachelor's, master's, & Ph.D. (depending on area of work)
Salary/Range:	$110,000 - $135,000

Minister of Religion/Clergyman

Leader and organizing church services or worship, conduct funerals, marriages, and other religious ceremonies; often provide spiritual guidance, counsel individuals, and moral support.

Education:	Bachelor's, master's, and Ph.D.
Salary/Range:	$85,000 - $125,000

Psychologist

Use various techniques, including interviews, psychological tests, and observations to diagnose and treat mental health conditions; helps individuals understand and manage their thoughts, feelings, and behaviors; ultimately improving their patients' overall wellbeing and quality of life.

Education:	Master's, Ph.D. degrees
Salary/Range:	$95,000 - $150,000

Political Lobbyist/Former member of Congress

Communicates or influences governing policy makers to support or oppose legislative laws or administrative regulations on behalf of their clients' interests, such as business leaders, labor unions, and non-profit organizations, on specific issues.

Education:	Bachelor's and master's degrees
Salary/Range:	$250,000 - $350,000

FINANCE PROFESSIONS

Financial Manager Controller

Oversees all accounting functions in a business enterprise or government agency, ensuring accurate financial reporting, compliance with regulations, maintenance of financial records; often creates annual budget, revenue policy, and forecasting, internal controls, and tracks accounting and budget departments.

Education:	Master's degree, Certified Public Accountant (CPA)
Salary/Range:	130,00,000 - $150,000

Certified Public Accountant/Auditors

Conduct financial and tax auditing, manage and prepare tax records, and perform forensic accounting for business enterprises, government agencies, and private individuals.

Education:	Master's degrees, CPA license
Salary/Range:	$120,000 - $200,000

Budget Analyst

Creating, analyzing, and managing budgets for organizations, while monitoring spending and making recommendations to improve financial health, forecasting future needs, and ensuring that spending aligns with organizational goals.

Education:	Bachelor's, master's degree
Salary/Range:	$90,000 - $120,000

Procurement Analyst

Evaluates and selects goods and service providers, negotiates contracts, and analyzes costs to optimize the company's purchasing process. Identify cost-saving opportunities, inventory quality control, ensure compliance with regulations, and maintain a professional relationship with vendors.

Education:	Bachelor's, master's degrees
Salary/Range:	$98,000 - $127,000

Financial Analyst

Analyzes financial data, makes projections, and provides financial recommendations to organizations to increase performance, manage financial risk, and make informed decisions based on economic conditions.

Education:	Master's degree, Certification License: Chartered Financial Analyst (CFA)
Salary/Range:	$110,000 - $150,000

Portfolio Manager

Managing investments for clients or organizations, analyzing economic conditions, following market data and trends, making strategic investment decisions to achieve specific financial goals, creating and managing investment strategies, and ensuring compliance with regulations

Education:	Bachelor's, master's degrees/Chartered Financial Analyst certification
Salary/Range:	$95,000 - $155,000

Registered Investment Adviser (RIA)

Providing financial advice, managing portfolios, ensuring compliance with regulatory standards, and developing a suitable financial plan based on clients' goals.

Education:	Bachelor's and master's degrees, licensed by FINRA (Financial Industry Regulatory Authority)
Salary/Range:	$109,000 - $115,000

Financial Adviser

Advising clients on investment strategies, retirement planning, and other financial matters; managing client portfolios, educating clients on financial products and services, following market trends; complying with regulations, and generating new clients.

Education:	Bachelor's, master's degrees/Certified Financial Planner (CFP)
Salary/Range:	$100,000 - $130,000

Personal Financial Advisors

Helping individuals with their financial planning, investments, taxes, insurance, and retirement, often assess economic condition, analyze clients' risk tolerance, make suitable financial adjustments, and provide ongoing support to ensure clients are on track to meet their financial goals.

Education:	Bachelor's, master's degrees, license by FINRA
Salary/Range:	$152,000 - $240,000

Financial Technologist/FinTech Specialist

Focuses on developing and implementing technology solutions to enhance financial processes and services, designing digital banking platforms, creating algorithms for automated trading, building secure systems for managing financial data, and blending technical skills like coding, data analysis, and systems architecture models.

Education:	Bachelor's and master's degrees in computer science and financial modeling
Salary/Range:	$125,000 - $180,000

Financial Software Developer

Involves designing, developing, and maintaining software applications used in the finance industry; creating software for various financial functions like credit, payment processing, and fraud detection; often works on projects that require a deep understanding of both programming and financial concepts.

Education:	Bachelor's, master's degree
Salary/Range:	$120,000 - $190,000

Financial Data Scientist

Analyze complex financial data, identify trends, predict market behavior, and make informed decisions within financial, designing algorithms for trading, analyzing customer data, building predictive models, and ensuring regulatory compliance.

Education:	Bachelor's and master's degrees in computer science and financial modeling
Salary/Range:	$110,000 - $135,000

Financial/Banking Examiner

Involves assessing financial health and compliance of financial institutions, often balance sheets, income and expenses, lending practices, loan levels risk, analyzing bank management to ensure adherence to laws and regulations.

Education:	Bachelor's, master's degrees/Examiner financial certification
Salary/Range:	$90,000 - $170,000

Quantitative Analyst

Use mathematical and statistical methods to analyze financial data and make informed decisions; develop and implement models for risk management, pricing, and investment strategies, often working with large datasets and algorithms to extract profitable trades.

Education:	Bachelor's, master's, and Ph.D. degrees
Salary/Range:	$125,000 - $201,000

Cybersecurity Specialist

Protect an organization's digital assets from cyber threats and vulnerabilities; responsible for identifying and mitigating security risks, implementing security measures, and responding to security issues.

Education:	Bachelor's, master's degree
Salary/Range:	$95,000 - $155,000

Investment Banker

Help clients such as corporations, government agencies, and private institutional investors raise financial capital like bonds, private stock offerings, mergers and acquisitions (M&A), and initial public offerings (IPO) to implement a strategic plan.

Education:	Bachelor's, master's degree
Salary/Range:	$175,000 - $500,000

Private Equity Portfolio Manager

Identifying potential investment opportunities by analyzing industries and economic market conditions; raising financial capital, conducting due diligence, determining appropriate valuations of business, and tracking financial performance of investments.

Education:	Bachelor's, master's degree (economics, finance, or law)
Salary/Range:	$150,000 - $500,000

Venture Capitalist (VC)

Invest in a startup company, often in exchange for a percentage of company equity, with the aim of achieving high returns through the company's potential growth; provide funds and strategic support to scale and maximize profits. Conduct due diligence, building a partnership network to raise financial capital.

Education:	Bachelor's, master's degree
Salary/Range:	$140,000 - $ Millions

Hedge Fund Analyst/Trader

Involves researching, analyzing, and evaluating investment opportunities often within a specific industry and making recommendations to the portfolio manager; also monitors risk, tracks market trends, and portfolio performance.

Education:	Bachelor's, master's degree in economics/financial modeling
Salary/Range:	$150,000 - $190,000 plus bonus

Hedge Fund Portfolio Manager

Generally, focuses on building and managing investment portfolios to achieve high returns, managing risk, communicating with investors, researching investment opportunities, staying up to date with market conditions, trends, and regulatory compliance.

Education:	Bachelor's, master's, and or Ph.D. in finance, math, economics, etc.
Salary/Range:	$350,000 - $550,000

Stock Broker/Trader

Buy and sell stocks on behalf of clients, ensuring the best possible prices. Provide investment advice, act as an intermediary between clients and the stock exchange, and analyze clients' needs and recommend appropriate investments.

Education:	Bachelor's, master's degree/state license
Salary/Range:	$140,000 - $195,000

Bond and Commodities Broker/Trader

Buying and selling commodities and bonds on behalf of clients; analyzing market conditions; providing investment advice and executing trades; earning commissions from successful transactions; building relationships with clients and institutional investors, and often managing clients' portfolios.

Education:	Bachelor's, master's degree
Salary/Range:	$105,000 - $150,000

Insurance Broker/Agent

Act as an intermediary between insurance buyers and insurance companies; provide insurance coverage as per the client's needs, budget, and legal requirements.

Education:	Bachelor's degree and state license (property, auto, life, and health).
Salary/Range:	$95,000 - $110,000

Mortgage Banker/Broker

Originates, underwrites, and often services mortgage loans on behalf of a lending institution; helps home buyers secure a mortgage loan; ensures that the loan is properly secured and qualified.

Education:	Bachelor's, master's degree
Salary/Range:	$110,000 - $135,000

Risk Manager

Identify, assess, and mitigate potential risks that could undermine an organization's day-to-day operation, often its finances and reputation; develop and implement risk management strategies, policies, and procedures to minimize threats and ensure compliance with regulations.

Education:	Bachelor's, master's degrees, and industry certification
Salary/Range:	$125,000 - $155,000

Credit Analysts

Analyze financial statements, credit reports, and other relevant information to assess borrowers' ability to repay; analyze financial data, assess risks, and make recommendations for loan approval or credit limits.

Education:	Bachelor's, master's degree, and industry certification.
Salary/Range:	$90,000 - $140,000

Underwriter Manager

Outlines responsibilities for leading and managing an underwriting team, ensuring compliance with company policies, and driving business growth through effective risk assessment and decision making; setting underwriting standards, and collaborating with other departments to achieve business objectives.

Education:	Bachelor's, master's/certification endorsement in insurance and financial risk
Salary/Range:	$135,000 - $175,000

Information Security Analyst

Analyze security risks, develop and implement security measures, and respond to computer security breaches; collaborate with various teams and educate employees on cyber security best practices. Troubleshoot security issues and develop effective solutions

Education:	Bachelor's, master's degree in a computer security-related field
Salary/Range:	$120,000 - $143,000

Financial and Investment Analysts

Involves providing guidance and insights to businesses and individuals on various types of investment strategies and decisions to maximize profits; evaluating financial data, market trends, and economic conditions to forecast future performance and recommendations; often evaluating potential financial risks associated with various decisions and proposing strategies to mitigate risks.

Education:	Bachelor's, master's degrees in the field of finance and economics, Chartered Financial Analyst (CFA) certification
Salary/Range:	$140,000 - $175,000

Financial Risk Analyst

Identifying financial risk to an organization or potential risks associated with investments, market conditions, credit, and operations; developing and implementing solutions to mitigate potential risk; proficiency in software tools that include financial modeling and data analysis platforms.

Education:	Bachelor's, master's degree in financial risk management, Various types of certifications: Certified Risk Manager (CRM), Financial Risk Manager (FRM), Professional Risk Manager (PRM), Chartered Enterprise Risk Analyst (CERA)
Salary/Range:	$116,000 - $175,000

LEGAL PROFESSIONS

Corporate Attorney

Provides legal advice and guidance to businesses and corporations, encompassing various aspects of operations; assists with matters ranging from contract drafting and legal compliance to handling legal disputes and advising on mergers and acquisitions; plays a role in risk management and ensuring companies navigate the complex legal environment.

Education:	Bachelor's, law degree, license, and training in a related field
Salary/Range:	$165,000 - $215,000

Constitutional Attorney

Involves cases related to the interpretation and application of the constitution, often representing individuals or groups in dispute cases against the government or when constitutional rights are violated; extensive knowledge of constitutional law; responsibilities also include research, drafting legal documents, preparing cases for court, and representing clients in legal proceedings. (civil right, criminal, appellate, and litigation cases)

Education:	Bachelor's, law degree, and Juris Doctor (J.D.)
Salary/Range:	$105,000 - $135,000

Prosecutor Attorney (aka District Attorney)

Represent the government in criminal cases, seeking to prove the defendant's guilt and ensure justice is served; determining charges, negotiating plea deals, presenting evidence in court, and advocating for appropriate sentences.

Education:	Bachelor's, law degrees, Juris doctor, state license, often internship/clerkships
Salary/Range:	122.000 - $160,000

Criminal Defense Attorney

Represents defendants in court proceedings, ensuring their rights are protected and providing a vigorous legal defense; gathers evidence, interview witnesses, and prepare defense strategy, often negotiating plea deals with prosecutors; advocate for client's best interests throughout the legal process.

Education:	Bachelor's, law degree, Juris Doctor (JD), state license
Salary/Range:	$105,000 - $125,000

Bankruptcy Attorney

Involves representing individuals or businesses in bankruptcy proceedings, advising clients on their options for debt relief, and guiding them through the legal process; preparing and filing court documents, attending hearings, negotiating with creditors, handling any litigation that may arise; assisting clients in rebuilding credit after bankruptcy discharge.

Education:	Bachelor's, law degree, license, and training in a related field
Salary/Range:	$187,000 - $250,000

Civil Litigation Attorney

Focus on civil disputes and initiate legal proceedings, conducting legal research in support of cases, drafting legal documents or petitions, requesting hearings, trials, depositions, and mediation, etc.; communicating with clients throughout the litigation process, and opposing counsel, staying up to date on legal modifications and legal strategies; negotiating settlement and resolution.

Education:	Bachelor's, law degree (JD), state license
Salary/Range:	$150,000 - $175,000

Security, Merger, and Acquisition Attorney

Focus on formulate buy sell securities document preparation and execution, advise clients like corporations, government agencies, or private institutions on compliance with security rules or regulations set by the Security and exchange commission (SEC) and/or FINRA; Rules that govern securities activities such as mergers and acquisitions, private placements, initial public offerings, bonds (debt financing) and litigation related investment, etc.

Education:	Bachelor's, law degree, license, and training in a related field
Salary/Range:	$120,000 - $180,000

Employment Attorney

Advise employers on employment laws, human resources on best practices, employee-related law; represent matters such as discrimination, harassment, wrongful termination, wage and hour disputes, etc., draft or review employment contracts, and handle cases before administrative agencies like EEOC

Education:	Bachelor's, law degree (JD), state license
Salary/Range:	$159,000 - $178,000

Entertainment Attorney

Advise clients on entertainment-related contracts, intellectual property, and business arrangements such as talent agreements, production deals, and licensing agreements like copyrights, trademarks, and rights of product distribution; often include regulatory compliance, financing, and investment agreements.

Education:	Bachelor's, law degree (JD), state license
Salary/Range:	$121,000 - $278,000

Tax Attorney

Provides legal counsel to individuals and businesses on various tax matters, including income tax, estate tax, corporate tax, and international tax; additionally, represents clients dealing with federal and state tax authorities in cases such as audits, disputes, settlements, litigation, etc.

Education:	Bachelor's, law degree (JD), state license
Salary/Range:	$127,000 - $217,000

Estate Planning Attorney

Provide clients with estate plans on distributing assets such as real estate, currency, insurance proceeds, stocks, etc. and ensuring desires are implemented after being unable to make decisions or have deceased; often involves drafting living wills, trusts, health care proxy, and other documents; advise on estate taxes, probate, estate trustee (s)/administrator, etc.

Education:	Bachelor's, law degree (JD), state license
Salary/Range:	$135,000 - $175,000

Intellectual Property Attorney (IP)

Specializes in protecting intangible assets like inventions, creative works, designs, and brand names; advises clients on IP rights, navigates complex IP laws, represents clients in disputes, ensuring the protection and enforcement of intellectual property.

Education:	Bachelor's, law degree (JD), state license
Salary/Range:	$189,000 - $243,000

Family Attorney

Involves clients with legal matters that relate to family relationships like divorce, child custody, adoption, domestic violence cases; provides guidance on mediation, settlement agreements, court pleading, hearing, and case law to support clients' cases.

Education:	Bachelor's, law degree (JD), state license
Salary/Range:	$116,000 – $165,000

Immigration Attorney

Advise clients on various aspects of U S Immigration law; provide service to individuals and businesses to navigate the complexities of obtaining permanent residency status, citizenship, and other related immigration matters; prepare and file applications, represent clients in court, and ensure compliance with immigration laws.

Education:	Bachelor's, law degree, Juris Doctor, state license
Salary/Range:	$105,000 - $165,000

Personal Injury Attorney

Advise and represent individuals who have been injured due to someone else's negligence or carelessness; help clients pursue compensation for injuries, medical expenses, lost wages, and pain and suffering; investigate claims, gathering evidence such as police report, medical record, witness statement and other related documents, negotiating with insurance companies, and often represent clients in court.

Education:	Bachelor's, law degree (JD), and state license
Salary/Range:	$113,000 - $164,000

Real Estate Attorney

Provides guidance and representation in property transactions, including buying, selling, and leasing; drafts and reviews contracts, escrows clients' funds, conducts title searches, ensuring property title is free and clear from any encumbrances; handles disputes, advises clients on zoning, land use issues, and prepares closing documents.

Education:	Bachelor's, law degree (JD), state license
Salary/Range:	$147,000 - $180,000

International Law Attorney

Handles legal issues that transcend national and international cross-border business matters, focusing on regulatory disputes like human rights, representing multi-national corporations and nation states in the international criminal court; often speaks multiple languages, has knowledge in multiple legal systems, and international treaties such as trade, investment, and environmental issues. Often works with the United Nations, World Bank, and the World Trade Organization

Education:	Bachelor's, law degree (JD), and certification in international law, Master of Laws (LLM)
Salary/Range:	$110,000 - $125,000

Public Policy Attorney

Work to shape legislation and influence government policies; research, analyze, and advise businesses and institutions on legal, legislative, and policy matters; represent clients in court or before government agencies, focusing on public interest issues or lobbying to put in effect, improve, or oppose specific polices/regulatory laws.

Education:	Bachelor's, Juris Doctor (JD) degrees, state license
Salary/Range:	$135,000 - $175,000

Arbitrators (dispute resolution out of traditional court litigation)

Evaluate the merits of cases (as in banking, investment, construction, international trade, and or intellectual property), review contracts or evidence, witness and cross-examine, make recommendations on what is mutually suitable, and resolve based on existing contract clauses; ensuring legally sound and enforceable; facilitating negotiations, settlement, etc.

Education:	Bachelor's, law degree (JD), state license
Salary/Range:	$120,000 - $131,000

Hearing Officers

Presides over hearings, similar to a judge, to make decisions or recommendations regarding disputes or claims; writes clear and concise decisions based on findings of fact and conclusions of law.

Education:	Bachelor's, law degree (JD), state license
Salary/Range:	$104,000 - $172,000

Administrative Law Judge

A federal employee who presides over administrative hearings and adjudicates disputes within government agencies, often involving regulatory laws that relate to benefits, immigration, employment, or government contracts; issuing and rulings

Education:	Bachelor's, law degree (JD), state license, or Bachelor's degree in Administrative Law and open competitive exam with U.S. Office of Personnel Management (OPM)
Salary/Range:	$110,000 - $150,000

Magistrate Judge (Source: Legal Information Institute)

Handle tasks such as warrants, overseeing first appearances of criminal defendants, setting bail, administrative duties like civil cases, misdemeanors, and petty offenses trials; conduct dispute resolution through mediation; often make recommendations to the district judge on dispositive motions, and summary judgment, etc.

Education:	Bachelor's. law degree (JD), State license, practice law for five years
Salary/Range:	$195,000 - $220,000

Real Estate Title Recording/Abstractors Manager

Researching and documenting the history of property ownership, which includes deeds, mortgages, ownership transfers, court document filings such as violations, liens, building permits, and any title encumbrance, etc.

Education:	Bachelor's, law degree, state license
Salary/Range:	$110,000 - $141,000

Law Profession without being a Lawyer

Claim Adjuster

Investigate various types of claims for insurance companies such as property damage, liability, and personal injury, communicate with parties, work with attorneys, medical, police, fire, and other related experts; gather relevant evidence, assess damages, determine coverage, write reports that include the extent or value of loss.

Education:	Bachelor's degree, state license
Salary/Range:	$96,000 - $110,000

Compliance Officer

Ensures an organization and internal polices, identifying and mitigating compliance risks; develops policy, conducts audits and training, investigates potential violations to maintain ethical and legal integrity; often collaborating with other departments to ensure effective implementation of compliance programs

Education:	Bachelor's, master's degree/industry/institution certification
Salary/Range:	$110,000 - $165,000

Court Reporter

Take an accurate record of legal proceedings in hearings, trials, and depositions; use stenographic machines or voice recording devices to capture spoken words and other auditory cues in chronological order; record witnesses and exhibits; provide written transcription to authorized parties upon request.

Education:	National Court Reports Association (NCRA)/Registered Professional Reporter (RPR) exam/state license exam
Salary/Range:	$95,000 - $$112,000

Electronic Discovery Specialist

Manage, protect, and process electronic data within the legal system; work with law firms, corporations, or government agencies, collecting, processing, and producing electronic information in legal cases.

Education:	Bachelor's degree, certifications: Certified E-discovery Specialist (CEDS)
Salary/Range:	$90,000 - $100,000

Jury Consultant Specialist

Develop knowledge to analyze and predict the behavior and biases of potential jurors; jury selection, survey to understand the demographics, attitudes, and beliefs of potential jurors in a specific jurisdiction and case; selection aims to shape a narrative that resonates or persuade conviction and outcome.

Education:	Bachelor's, master's, and Ph.D. in social science or law degree
Salary/Range:	$95,000 - $150,000

Title Agent/Examiner

Ensures the transfer of property ownership by verifying the validity of the title and facilitating the closing process; researching public records, conducting and reviewing title documents, resolving title issues, and coordinating with buyer and seller attorneys involved in the transaction; facilitating the closing process, ensuring all necessary documentation is in order, and funds are properly disbursed.

Education:	Bachelor's degree in a related field such as estate, business, or paralegal studies Certification: America Land Title Association (ALTA) or National Title Professional (NTP) designation
Salary/Range:	$129,000 - $255,000

MANAGERIAL AND ADMINISTRATIVE CAREERS

Marketing/Sales Manager

Developing and implementing marketing strategies to promote a company's products or services through multiple media channels. For example, digital, print, social, television, and email.

Education:	Bachelor's, master's degree
Salary/Range:	$110,000 - $190,000

General Operation Manager

Oversees day-to-day operation of an organization, planning, directing, and coordinating operations across multiple departments or locations; formulating policies and utilizing human and financial resources to maximize revenue and performance efficiency.

Education:	Bachelor's, master's degrees/Certified Manager (CM)
Salary/Range:	$136,000 - $165,000

Advertising and Promotion Manager

Plans and coordinates advertising campaigns to increase sales of products or services; creates promotional materials like coupons to reach target audiences through various marketing channels such as radio, television, digital/social networks

Education:	Bachelor's, master's degree
Salary/Range:	$126,000 - $206,000

Marketing Manager

Developing and implementing marketing plan to promote company's products or services, build brand awareness to drive sales; research and analyze trend, identify target audiences across multi-channels such as new paper, digital, social media, and television; manage budget, track performance and adjust plan as needed to achieve maximum revenue results; build and maintain strong relationship with external partners;

Education:	Bachelor's, master's degree
Salary/Range:	$125,000 - $160,000

Public Relations Manager

Crafting and implementing communication strategies to build and maintain a positive public image for an organization or individual; working with journalists and media outlets to ensure a positive image of clients.

Education:	Bachelor's, master's degree, Certification: Accredited in Public Relations (CPRC)
Salary/Range:	$138,000 - $140,000

Sales Manager

Hire and train sales team, setting sales goals and quotas to achieve increasing revenue growth; identify target markets, provide coaching and feedback; foster a positive and productive team environment; identify trends, evaluate sales performance, make recommendations for improvements; research new territory, new sales channels, new strategies to maximize sales results.

Education:	Bachelor's, master's degrees (industry license, product sale certification)
Salary/Range:	$169,000 - $216,000

Fundraising Manager

Building and managing relationship with potential donors such as individuals, corporations, and foundations to secure financial support for an organization; drafting compelling messaging that aligns with vision and mission of the organization; recruiting, training, and managing volunteers to support fundraising efforts; track fund raising effort to see areas that need improvement and budget to ensure efficient resource allocation.

Education:	Certified Fund-Raising Executive (CFRE)
Salary/Range:	$110,000 - $135,000

Human Resource Manager

Plans and coordinates administrative functions within an organization, including recruiting, hiring, employee relations, payroll, training, employee performance records, and ensures compliance with laws and regulations; employees' benefits program such as health insurance, retirement plans.

Education:	Bachelor's, master's degrees, certification: Society of Human Resource Manager-Certified Professional (SHRM-CP) or SHRM-SCP (Senior Certified Professional)
Salary/Range:	$121,000 - $127,000

Compensation and Benefits Manager

Manages an organization's compensation and benefits programs to attract, retain, and motivate top talent; develops competitive pay structures that include bonus plans, health insurance, retirement plans, and training, etc.; provides clear and accurate information about programs and policies

Education:	Bachelor's, master's degrees in human resource/business administration/Society for Human Resource Management (SHRM) certification
Salary/Range:	$125,000 - $156,000

Training and Development Manager

Engage in employees' education, mentorship, and training management; designing and implementing training programs to improve employee skills, knowledge, and overall workforce productivity performance, while aligning with the organization's strategic human development goals;

Education:	Bachelor's, master's degrees, certified professional in learning and performance CPLP/certified professional in talent development (CPTD certification
Salary/Range:	$130,000 - $180,000

Administrative Services Manager

Plan, direct, and oversee various administrative services within an organization; develop new approaches to streamline day-to-day operations, prepare and manage budgets, increase revenue, and ensure cost control efficiency, such as supplies, equipment, and budget; implement polices and ensure regulatory compliance.

Education:	Bachelor's, master's degree in administrative management, certification: International Facility Management Association (IFMA), or Institute of Certified Records Managers (ICRM)
Salary/Range:	$110,000 - $137,000

Contract Administrator

Manages the contract lifecycle that includes drafting and negotiation to execution, tracking deadlines, renewals, and terminations; ensuring contracts perform to standards, monitoring regulatory requirements, and potential risk mitigation; ensuring accurate details and maintaining records, coordinating with other skilled professionals like lawyers, engineers, and accountants.

Education:	Bachelor's and master's degrees in related fields such as business law, finance, economics, and management; Certifications: Certified Federal Contracts Manager (CFCM) or Certified Professional Contracts Manager (CPCM)
Salary/Range:	$105,000 - $128,000

Computer Information Systems Manager

Responsible for planning and directing computer-related activities within an organization; oversees security and performance of information technology system infrastructure and systems such as server hardware and software applications.

Education:	Bachelor's, master's degrees in computer science/Computer Technology Industry Association (COMPTIA) certification.
Salary/Range:	$150,000 - $175,000

Financial Manager

Oversees and manages an organization's financial activities, such as financial reporting, budgeting, investment management, and ensuring compliance with financial regulations; develops and implements strategies to optimize financial performance, including financial risk, and identifies trends and opportunities.

Education:	Bachelor's, master's degrees in financial management and leadership; certification: Certified Financial Manager (CFM)
Salary/Range:	$135,000 - $204,000

Industrial Production Manager

Oversee and optimize the manufacturing process to ensure efficient and timely production of goods; day-to-day operations include material procurement to shipping of finished goods to customers; ensuring quality control, budget control, tracking market conditions, looking for areas for improvement, and safety and regulatory compliance

Education:	Bachelor's, master's degree in the related industry, and certification
Salary/Range:	$121,000 - $150,000

Education Administrative (Kindergarten through Secondary)

Often the principal or superintendent oversees the academic, administrative, and auxiliary activities of schools; ensures the school meets educational standards, manages budgets, provides teacher support and leadership; roles also include evaluating students and teachers' improvement programs, recruiting, hiring, training and collaborating with staff to develop curriculum.

Education:	Master's, Ph.D. degrees in administration and education leadership
Salary/Range:	$125,000 - $190,000

Education Administrator (Postsecondary)

Encompassing higher education policy and procedure management, budget, student and staff hiring, training, evaluating staff, curriculum development, and ensuring a safe and positive learning environment, compliance with educational standards and regulations.

Education:	Master's, Ph.D. degrees in administration and education leadership
Salary/Range:	$135,000 - $190,000

Architectural and Engineering Manager

Plan, coordinate, and oversee the development of building projects, ensuring required technical accuracy of design, standards, and regulations of development; ensure smooth workflow, budget over-run control, timely completion, hiring staff, reducing adverse environmental impact, etc.

Education:	Master's in engineering and management (MEM) or master of science in technology management (MSTM), state license
Salary/Range:	$165,000 - $240,000

Medical and Health Services Manager

Overall planning, coordination of medical and health services within a healthcare facility; ensuring efficient and safe delivery of medical services; budgeting, staffing, training, employee benefit programs, making sure of regulatory compliance and standards

Education:	Master's degree/M.D./Ph.D. in healthcare administration and management certification
Salary/Range:	$116,000 - $197,000

Natural Sciences Manager (relates to biology, chemistry, and physics)

Oversee scientific research, development-related activities; manage a team of scientists and technicians; ensure research is conducted accurately and efficiently; also engage in budget, research findings report, policy development, meeting project goals, standards, and regulatory compliance.

Education:	Master's and Ph.D. degrees and related certification
Salary/Range:	$160,000 - $320,000

POSTSECONDARY EDUCATORS

Post-secondary education is described as any further education that one pursues after high school. Post-secondary educators consist of a broad range of professionals who work within educational institutions or in fields that require advanced degrees or certifications.

These individuals teach in colleges, universities, vocational schools, continuing education, or life skills programs. Common examples are medical, law, finance, engineering, social science, etc.

English Language and Literature Professor

Develop curriculum in English language and literature; conduct lectures to college students in various aspects of English language and literature, including linguistics, comparative literature, and creative writing.

Education:	Bachelor's, master's, and Ph.D. degrees
Salary/Range:	$101,000 - $137,000

Mathematics Professor

Develop curriculum and lesson plan, teach various math courses, from introductory algebra to advanced graduate level mathematics

Education:	Bachelor's, master's, and Ph.D. degrees
Salary/Range:	$125,000 - $133,000

Economics Professor

Develop economic curriculum and lesson plan and lecture university students focusing on microeconomics and macroeconomics principles; often times, teach finance and specialize in labor economics.

Education:	Bachelor's, master's, and Ph.D. degrees
Salary/Range:	$150,000 - $209,000

Architecture Professor

Engage in educating students in architectural design that includes interior, exterior layout, landscape rendering, history, and theory; teach students how to design and develop building projects, lectures, and studio work, insights into developing, drafting details, and technical skills.

Education:	Bachelor's, master's, and Ph.D. degrees in related fields
Salary/Range:	$110,000 - $170,000

Engineering Professor

Engage in lectures that relate to civil, industrial, chemical, mechanical, and electrical engineer courses to undergraduate and graduate students; conduct research, supervise student research, and participate in departmental services activities at the university.

Education:	Bachelor's, master's, and Ph.D. degrees in related fields
Salary/Range:	$140,000 - $160,000

Biological Science Professor

Participate in curriculum development and course planning; deliver engaging lectures and laboratory sessions; design and administer exams, assignments, and research projects; mentor and advise students

Education:	Bachelor's, master's, and Ph.D. degrees in related fields
Salary/Range:	$230,000 - $300,000

Agricultural Sciences Professor

Conduct lectures and laboratory projects; class discussions on various crop production, plant genetics, and soil chemistry; additionally, fisheries production management, dairy science, and animals such as cows, pigs, chickens, etc.

Education:	Bachelor's, master's, and Ph.D. degrees in related fields
Salary/Range:	$90,000 - $110,000

Atmospheric and Space Professor

Develop and deliver college-level courses on atmospheric and space science that include weather forecasting, climate, and space conditions; conduct data collection in lab and outdoor research; and mentor students on career paths.

Education:	Bachelor's, master's, and Ph.D. degrees
Salary/Range:	$95,000 - $150,000

Physics Professor

Develop and deliver lectures and laboratory sessions; prepare course materials such as syllabi, lecture notes, and assignments; stay current with new advancements and incorporate new discoveries into lectures; guide student research projects; and provide mentoring and career opportunities.

Education:	Master's and Ph.D. degrees
Salary/Range:	$106,000 - $118,000

Chemistry Professor

Develop and deliver engaging and informative lectures to undergraduate and graduate students, update course material, grading assignments, and exams, and provide feedback to students; conduct research in various fields of chemistry.

Education:	Master's and Ph.D. degrees
Salary/Range:	$123,000 - $195,000

Anthropology and Archeology Professor

Develop and delivers lectures to college students in areas like cultural anthropology, archaeology, linguistics, and other related topics; assesses student work, provides and assigns course work materials like exams, and research projects on related subjects

Education:	Master's and Ph.D. degrees
Salary/Range:	$94,000 - $105,000

Ethnic and Cultural Studies Professor

Lectures about diverse cultures, ethnicities, and groups, often with a focus and power dynamics, social behavior, beliefs, and practices; conduct research on related topics, publish findings and observations; course work materials, assess students, and provide mentoring on career opportunities.

Education:	Master's and Ph.D. degrees
Salary/Range:	$90,000 - $110,000

Political Science Professor

Prepare and deliver lectures on various political science topics; facilitate and moderate classroom discussions, design and administer exams, provide course materials, and maintain student grades.

Education:	Master's and Ph.D. degrees
Salary/Range:	$95,000 - $127,000

Sociology Professor

Instruct undergraduate and graduate courses in various sociology topics; design, update, and maintain course syllabi and materials; grade student performance, administer exams, and provide students' feedback; have office hours to address students' private concerns.

Education:	Master's and Ph.D. degrees
Salary/Range:	$110,000 - $169,000

Health Specialties Professor

Teaches courses such as dentistry, medicine, and public health to students at undergraduate and graduate levels; develops and delivers lectures, creates course materials, assesses student work; mentoring students, participates in curriculum development, and engages in professional development.

Education:	Ph.D. degree in a related field
Salary/Range:	$150,000 - $239,000

Nursing Instructor

Designing and delivering educational materials, lesson plans, lectures, and learning activities for nursing students and staff; evaluating students' performance, guiding student clinical practice, providing feedback, and staying up to date with advancements in the nursing field.

Education:	Master's degree, Registered Nurse, Certified Nurse Educator (CNE), or Ph.D.
Salary/Range:	$122,000 - $168,000

History Professor

Develop and deliver lectures, create course material, grade assignments and student feedback, conduct research, and contribute to the academic community.

Education:	Master's and Ph.D. degrees
Salary/Range:	$102,00 - $106,000

Computer Science Professor

Preparing and delivering computer science lectures to college students, designing syllabi, materials, and project-related assignments, assessing student work, advising students on career paths, staying up to date with evolving computer advancement, and integrating them into course materials.

Education:	Master's and Ph.D. degrees
Salary/Range:	$126,000 - $171,000

Music Professor

Plan and implement music lessons, lecture on music theory, practical skills, and history of music, teach students to play music instruments, read and understand music as well as develop voice techniques; evaluate students' progress, prepare students for exams, auditions, and performances; often conduct choirs, orchestras, or bands.

Education:	Master's, Ph.D. degree, or Doctor of Musical Arts (DMA).
Salary/Range:	$108,000 - $113,000

Law Professor

Develop and lecture in specialized areas as civil, constitutional, intellectual property, international, environmental laws, etc.; facilitate discussions and assess students' understanding of material such as case law, stats, and legal protocols; often engage in students' mentoring program; grade students' performance, and advise students on career paths.

Education:	Master of Laws (LLM), Doctor of Juridical Science (S.J.D), or Ph.D. in law.
Salary/Range:	$167.000 – $198,000

Art, Drama, and Music Instructor

Teach courses in fine applied art drama, and music in colleges and universities students; deliver lectures, leading discussions and demonstrate artistic techniques; evaluate student performances and assignments; tutor, advise and guide students on academic or career directions; promote programs and manage department activities.

Education:	Master's, and Ph.D. degrees in related field
Salary/Range:	$108,000 - $110,000

Philosophy and Religion Professor

Develop lecture materials, conduct lectures to college students; facilitate classroom discussion on philosophy, religion, and theology; engage students in critical thinking; grade assignments and exams.

Education:	Master's and Ph.D. degrees
Salary/Range:	$104,000 - $119,000

Criminal Justice and Law Professor

Develop and lecture college students on the criminal justice system, law enforcement, corrections, and judicial process; engaging in classroom discussions, assessing student work assignments, exams, research papers, and updating course materials.

Education:	Master's and Ph.D. degrees in criminal law
Salary/Range:	$129,000 - $200,000

Communication Professor

Teaches communication courses to college and university students in media studies, journalism, or related fields; develops and conducts lectures, assesses overall performance, and mentors students, incorporating new technologies and trends into their teaching.

Education:	Master's and Ph.D. degrees
Salary/Range:	$108,000 - $120,000

General Education Teacher

Imparting knowledge, facilitating learning, and fostering students' overall development; guides, mentors, encourage students to analyze information, think critically, and solve problems, creating positive learning environments, and adapting teaching methods to meet individual student needs; subjects include mathematics, English language, science, and social studies, etc.

Education:	Master's and Ph.D. degree in a related field
Salary/Range:	$83,000 - $127,000

ENTREPRENEURSHIP

In the context of macro-economics, the three components that describe the economy are entrepreneurs, who build businesses to produce and distribute their goods or services; consumers who use the goods produced or the services offered; and government institutions that provide public services, regulatory policies as guardrails for business enterprises and consumers.

The **focus here is entrepreneurship. So, what kind of people are entrepreneurs, and where do they come from?** According to Open A.I., Entrepreneurs can be described as individuals who identify an unmet need in their communities. Having an achievement motive, they develop innovative solutions for the community, and as they grow, they expand across different communities. The innovation framework includes organizing the best human capital, technological/financial capital, and land space. In essence, it is vision and passion to build from the ground up, the courage to see beyond risk and challenges, the drive to succeed, and the prospect to advance their lives, investors, employees, and their consumers' living standard. Entrepreneurs play an important role in the income growth of households and the overall national growth of the economy. The other crucial benefit of entrepreneurship is the innovative products and services that they produce, which allow society to advance in living standards. Entrepreneurship research and technological development carry society from the past and into the current level of modernity, like development of mobile communication, healthcare, robots, television, transportation, tools and convenient of all type, etc.

Entrepreneurs bring new ideas to the market and oftentimes challenge established companies with new opportunities for a new type of employment and economic growth. Another benefit of entrepreneurship is the multiplier effect. In other words, one entrepreneur's business enterprise has the supportive need for many other business services or products. As this situation expands employment into other parts of the economy, it increases consumer spending and tax revenue that allow the government to provide better services. On many occasions, the demand for workers increases; and as a result, the need for more housing and community services increases. Besides, entrepreneurship provides other benefits such as long-term employment, social and economic stability of communities.

Consider the various natural resources that have been discovered, such as oil, natural gas, and rare earth materials. When these types of resources are coupled with financial capital and human ingenuity, this combined effort provides long-term economic growth and a high standard of living for the decade to come. These initiatives require the collaboration of entrepreneurs and supportive government policies in research and development. These discoveries often lead to the production of many different consumer products, which increases economic activity. Moreover, these developments often lead to structural change as well as social and economic adoption of the new technologies. Often new technological innovation not only creates new industries, but it also rejuvenates many of the old industries, which see the benefit to upgrade their organizational goods or services. Consequently, society benefits overall. In support of this discussion, let's look at a few examples of products that derive from oil and gas, also known as petrochemicals and rare earth materials.

List of finished goods and services used daily:

Oil	Natural Gas	Rare Earth Materials
Heating Homes	Heating Homes	Smart Phones
Gasoline	Cooking	Computer Hardware
Lubricants	Place Of Business	Flat Television Screens
Jet Fuel	Transportation	Fluorescent Lights

Oil	Natural Gas	Rare Earth Materials
Paving Roads	Air Conditioners/Refrigeration Plants	Medical X-Ray Tubes/MRI Device
Paint	Electrical Power Generation Plant	Electronics Components
Plastics Fibers	Manufacturing Paper, Glass, Steel	Batteries
Gloves, Plastic Bags, Face Masks	Fertilizer	Magnets
Medical Intravenous Line	Cosmetics	Led Lights
Petroleum Jelly Oil	Welding Gas	Wind Turbines, Solar Panels
Candles	Sulfur	Glass

The second part of the question is, "From where do entrepreneurs come? According to W. Lloyd Warner, author of *Social Class in America,* conclusive studies have shown that fifty to eighty percent of business leaders in the United States and across the world come from lower-upper class to middle upper-class backgrounds. It is where the mindset of parents is clear about the value of education. Many of whom may have some college education. They understand and value the social and economic mobility, as well as the process of cultivating and nurturing a high-achievement mindset in their children. Warner further argued that individuals from lower-upper class who focus on their personal growth, discipline themselves to acquire high income careers or build business that allow them to transition into middle class and often times, upper middle class of society. The individuals from upper middle class with high desire for achievement motive also choose high income careers or build business which advance them into upper class. When parents are clear about high value education, the value of high-income careers, as well as the process of. economic mobility, they tend to cultivated and nurtured a high-achievement mindset in their children.

It is those individuals with a set of cultural values who are driven to succeed in their educational pursuits and careers who become business leaders. Given their ambition and hunger for success, a number of individuals forego completing Ivy League universities to focus on their vision and passion. Many have not only become captains of industries, but they have also changed the world for the better. Steve Jobs built Apple; Bill Gates built Microsoft; Mark Zuckerberg built Facebook Social Network, renamed as Meta. Michael Dell built Dell computers. Ralph Lauren built the Ralph Lauren clothing line, Quincy Jones, an American record producer, composer, and arranger, Larry Ellison built Oracle, a computer software company, Richard Bronson, Virgin Atlantic, and so many others. The world is waiting for your idea. What will you build?

MASTERY

Mastery is the development of skills, special abilities, or the capability to fashion ideas and materials into what you desire. In other words, mastery is the ability to achieve the highest level of skill or expertise in a particular career. Every individual has the natural potential within to master his vocational pursuits if he learns the secrets of the field he chosen; submit to rigorous apprenticeship, absorb the hidden knowledge possessed by those with years of experience; and not only build on top of the layer of knowledge found; but to surge beyond and established new pattern and standards from the creative mind.

In fact, every time you change careers or acquire new skills, you reenter this critical phase where you have to learn from the experienced individuals in that field or experience the pain of self-apprenticeship. The process of self-apprenticeship is slow and, at first, can be very frustrating because you will fail over and over, which is painful. You will, at times, experience self-doubt due to a lack of clarity as to getting the result you want. This is where you must have discipline and determination for your vision to materialize. As you evolve, you will ultimately develop the necessary skills, the resolve to transform yourself into an independent thinker, and be prepared for the creative challenges on the way to mastery. The selection of your career should have the association with high financial reward and prestige.

Think of Steve Jobs, who had the vision to not only pioneer, but to revolutionize the world with the personal computer, mobile telephone, and digital music, or Henry Ford with the automobile. But there were many twists and turns in their journey to success. After many years of building Apple, Steve Jobs was forced out of Apple by the board of directors. Steve moved on to build another company, Pixar/NeXT Computer. But later, the board of directors decided to acquire Steve's new companies, Pixar/NeXT, and reappoint Steve Jobs back to run Apple as he sees fit. Apple became one of America's most successful companies. So, one can conclude that the pain that Steve experienced was there not only to teach him lessons, but was also part of the process to learn, grow, and lead. You must prepare to contend with human nature, which is at the center of your apprenticeship journey. Objectively, human character, which is often driven by envy, conformism, rigidity, self-obsessiveness, lack of discipline, flightiness, and passive aggression, is one of many human traits that make up the human spirit. The journey of success requires a strong sense of awareness as it relates to adaptability, humility, self-accountability, and imagination are just a few of the values you need to succeed.

In the second example of Henry Ford, according to Ford's biographer Robert Lacey, Ford was an apprentice machinist. He was fascinating with mechanics and spent much of his spare time experimenting with engines. He was hired as an engineer by the Edison Illuminating Company. Ford decided to pursue his passion for building gasoline engines. Ford organized the Detroit Automobile Company, which went bankrupt some eighteen months later. Even though Henry failed, he believed in his vision to build an automobile. After building prototypes such as the quadricycle and sweepstakes, a version for racing, Ford concluded the best version would be an eight-cylinder vehicle. But his engineers thought that it was impossible to make a gasoline engine. After many backs and forth with his team and investors, Henry Ford was able to reshape their beliefs that his vision was possible.

So, with his clear conviction, high innovative spirit, and dedication to pioneer an automobile industry, Henry Ford founded the Ford Motor Company with his high achievement motive to revolutionize the production of affordable automobiles for the world. Many potential investors thought that no one would want to use this type of transportation; the lack of road infrastructure was not in place, and workers assembled in line were discontent. But Ford believed that he would transform people's lives, and sure, he did. In 1946, Henry Ford was lauded at the automotive Golden Jubilee for contributions to the automotive industry, where over fifty thousand people cheered. Later that year, the American Petroleum Institute awarded him its first Gold Medal annual award for outstanding contributions to the welfare of humanity.

I have cited various attributes in my introduction page #. Nevertheless, here in my closing remarks, as you evolve in your entrepreneurship journey, you will discover that having the ambition for high achievement, you are required to have a higher level of intention and awareness in intelligence and skills. You will need to develop the mental fortitude to *focus*, build *self-confidence*, and *imagination*. And most crucially, *fact-based thinking*, and the ability to gain from temporary failure. Let us put these abilities in context. Focus is the ability to concentrate your effort on a central idea or task. For the use of a welding torch that burns through steel, consistent drops of water that bore holes in granite rock, or the energy of the sun shining on a magnified glass can start a fire. In other words, focus is one of the key ingredients for success. *Self-confidence* is the ability to examine your identity and organize your strengths and weaknesses into two buckets. First, you will concentrate on your strength, and second, you outsource to highly capable individuals where you are weak.

It is a well-known fact that modernity in society is built on imagination. *Imagination* is the action of forming new ideas, planning, and developing new processes and systems. You must force yourself to develop a strong sense of *imagination* because it is the lifeblood of human creativity and achievement. *Fact-based thinking* is one of the most critical abilities that you need for success. In other words, being able to gather and organize facts on which to base your thinking so as to make the right decision. Finally, success is not just for the select few, but also for the individuals who are committed to their lifelong personal growth.

I believe that one of the best ways to inspire young children is through stores; positive, realistic, and inspiring children's storybooks. See the following list below:

- **What Will You Be?**
  By Yamile S. Mendez: What will you be when you grow up? A young girl dreams about all the endless possibilities, sparking a sense of wonder, curiosity, and growth. With her abuela's (grandmother's) loving guidance, she learns her potential is limitless.

- **Moving Up!**
  By Rosemary Wells: Susannah wants to be a pilot, Akiko a doctor or nurse, Amanda a teacher, and Rafa a mechanic. They all had special talents when they were in kindergarten that sparked their dreams. This celebratory picture book will inspire readers, too.

- **In You I See**
  By **Rachel Emily:** "In You I see" highlights and celebrate the colorful layers in all of us. With enthralling, rhyming text by singer, songwriter Rachel "Maiday" Moulden, this enchanting children's storybook brings the magic of rhyme and nature together.

- **What Do You Do with a Chance?**
  By **Kobi Yamada:** A captivating story about a child who isn't sure what to make of a chance encounter. They discover that when you have courage, take chances, and say yes to new experiences, amazing things can happen.

- **What Would You Do in a Book About You?**
  By **Jean Reidy:** No dream is too big or too small in this heartwarming book about you. An exuberant tale that asks what wonderful, endless possibilities your story and your future might hold, making you the author of your own powerful story.

- **All Because You Matter**
  By **Tami Charles:** This lyrical, heart-lifting love letter to Black and Brown children everywhere reminds them how much they matter, that they have always mattered and always will.

- **Are You Ready? The World is Waiting**
  By Eric Carle: It's time for you to spread your wings and fly. The world can seem like a scary place. But you are ready. Bold illustrations and easy-to-read text encourage children who are going out into the world to spread their wings, knowing they have the drive to succeed.

- **The Wonderful Things You Will Be**
  By Emily W. Martin: Charming illustrations and simple, rhyming text reveal a parent's musings about what a child will become, knowing that the child's kindness, cleverness, and boldness will shine through no matter what.

- **I Believe I Can**
  By Grace Byers: I believe I Can is an affirmation for boys and girls of every background to love and believe in themselves. A new classic that's the perfect gift for baby showers, birthdays, or just for reading at home again and again.

- **I Am Every Good Thing**
  By Derrick Barnes: The confident narrator of this book is proud of everything that makes him who he is. He's got big plans, and I doubt he'll see them through. Illustrations and easy-to-read text pay

homage to the strength, character, and worth of a child.

- **When I Grow Up**
  By Julie Chen: One night, while getting ready for bed, a little boy starts to wonder what life would be like when I grow up. He tells his mother all about his big ideas. But when exactly will he grow up? And why does it take so long?

- **Just in Case You Want to Fly**
  By Julie Fogliano: funny and sweet, told with lyrical text and bright, unexpected illustrations, "Just in Case you Want to Fly" is a celebration of heading off on new adventures, and of knowing your loved ones will always have your back when you need them.

- **Tomorrow I'll Be Brave**
  By Jessica Hische: Journey through a world filled with positivity, with beautifully hand-lettered words of wisdom, inspiration, and motivation. As this book reminds readers, tomorrow is another day, full of endless opportunities.

BIBLIOGRAPHY

Warner W. Lloyd, Meeker, Eells. 1960, Social Class in America, Chicago, Harper Torch Book

McClelland, C. David. 1961, The Achieving Society. Princeton, NJ: D. Van Nostrand Comp. First Press

Perez, Carlota. Technological Revolutions and Financial Capital. MA, 2003 Edward Elgar Publishing.

https://careersinmedicine.aamc.org/explore-options/specialty-profiles

The American Finance Association Career/Directory

Joosephson, Mattew. Edison: A biography. New York: John Wiley & Son, Inc 1992

Atkinson, J. W. & Miller, D. R. Parent experiences in child training

Behavioral Research Service, Motive patterns of managers and specialists, New York; General Electric Company 1960

Bradburn, N. M. & Berlew, D. E. Need for Achievement and English economic growth. Economic Development change 1961 in press

Cole, A. H. Entrepreneurship and economic growth, Mimeographed. Cambridge, Mass.: Social Science Research Council and Harvard University

Litwin, G. H. Achievement motivation, social class, and the slope of occupational preferences in the United States and Japan. Dittoed paper. Dept of Social Relations, Harvard University, 1959

Rostow, W. W. The process of economic growth. New York: Noron, 1952.

US Bureau of Labor & Statistics/Occupational Employment & Wage Statistics Directory

https://www.americanbar.org/careercenter/career-choice-series/archive/

Smith, A. An inquiry into the nature and causes of the wealth of nations. 1776 New York Random House, 1937

McCelland, D. C. Risk-taking in children with high and low need for achievement. Princeton, N. J.: Van Nostrand, 1958

McCelland D. C., & Bradburn, N. M Achievement and managerial success, Dittoed paper. Harvard University 1957

McClelland Talent and society. Princeton, N. J.: Van Nostrand 1958, pages 135-194

Warner, W. L., & Abegglen, J. C. Occupational Mobility in American business and Industry. Minneapolis University of Minnesota Press, 1955

Weber, M. The Protestant ethic and the spirit of capitalism. 1904. New York: Scribner, 1930

Whiting, J. W. M, & Child, Child training and personality. New Haven, Conn.: Yale University Press1953

Silbiger, Steven. The Jewish Phenomenon. 2009 Evans, M. Rowman & Littlefield Publishing, Maryland

Occupational Outlook Handbook by US Bureau of labor & Statistics

Strodtbeck, F. L., McDonald, M. R., & Rosen, B. Evaluation of occupation: a reflection of Jewish and Italian mobility differences. Amer, social. Rev., 1957 pgs:22,546-553

Winterbottom, Marian R. The relation of need for achievement to learning experiences in independence and mastery. J. W. Atkinson

Kuhn, Thomas S. The Structure of Scientific Revolutions. Chicago, IL: The University of Chicago Press, 1996

Watts, Steven. The People's Tycoon: Henry; Ford and the American century. New York: Vintage Books, 2006

Open A I Search, Forage/blog/Careers

Storr, Anthony. The Dynamics of Creation. New York; Ballantine Books, 1993

Sowell, Thomas, Ethnic America, Basic Books, 1981 pg. 5.

Karp, Abraham, A History of the Jews in America, Jason Aronson, Inc., 1997

Wilder, Esther, and Walters, William, Journal of Economic & Social Measurement, 1997. Pg. 198

Rosenberg, Roy, Everything You Need to Know about America's Jews and Their History, Plume, 1997, pg.215

Hirschman, Elizabeth, American Jewish Ethnicity: Its Relationship to Some Selected Aspects of Consumer Behavior, Journal of Marketing, summer 1981, pg.102

Sanders, Adriemme, On My Mind: Success Secrets of the Successful, Forbes, November 2, 1998, pg. 22

The Ten-Day MBA: A Step-by-Step Guide to Mastering the Skills Taught in America's Top Business Schools, Harper Collins 2005

Redfield, Robert. 1950. A Village That Choose Progress. Chicago: University of Chicago Press.

Wrigt, Louis, ed. 1958 Middle Class Culture in Elizabethan England, Ithaca, N Y Cornell University Press

Castells, Manuel, vol. 1. 1996 vol2 1997 The Information Age, Economy, Society and Culture, Oxford: Blackwell.

Chandler, Alfred D. 1997 The Visible Gand; The Managerial Revolution in American Business, Cambridge, MA and London: Havard University Press.

Chick, Virginia 1992, The Evolution of Banking System and The Theory of saving, Investment and Interest, P. and Dow, S.C. eds, On Money Method: Keynes, Macmillan, pgs.193-205

INDEX

F

Financial Professions

S

Social Science Professions